Dark Days

by

Sue Hammond

Chapter One –
The beginning of the end

I loved him so much, but I knew I couldn't hold on to him. He had been my husband, confidant and support for thirty-four years. We had been through so much together and he was the kindest man you could ever meet.

We sat and listened to the doctor in the hospital and I stopped breathing, tears rolling down my face. I knew then that he was going to leave me.

Incurable. Non-operational. It won't respond to chemo. Those are all the words I took in.

Jeff took my hand and I will never forget his words: "I've had a brilliant life. I'm ready to go."

Then came the disbelief and anger. He was only seventy-two and he was fit as a fiddle; cycling, walking and his favourite pastime, rowing. He didn't smoke, apart from a very occasional cigar, and drank in moderation.

For twelve months he had been seeing our local GP about pains in his stomach and as he previously had bowel cancer he was concerned. He was reassured time and time again that it was probably IBS. Now we were sat in a hospital room being told he had pancreatic cancer and was inoperable.

We drove home in silence and I immediately went sick from my job as a housing officer to care for him. We both knew there wasn't a lot of time left but never actually said it. I wish we had. I wish we had sat down and faced it together, but we couldn't do it.

If I convinced myself it wasn't happening, maybe it wouldn't.

The hardest job was to tell our two children. We had always been a close family and it was heart breaking to see them so upset.

Over the next few weeks Jeff continued to lose weight and his powerful muscles turned to flab.

I took on the full responsibility of the house and garden which was physically hard work. Jeff tried to help, and I knew it was killing him watching me doing everything.

In hindsight I wish I hadn't tried to keep so busy. If I wasn't in the garden I was de-cluttering the shed or garage. I know he slept a lot, but we should have talked more. Talked about our feelings. Talked about our memories. The children. His life! Also, about the more mundane stuff like finances, housing issues, direct debits, insurance companies, etc etc. He had always dealt with this stuff.

I guess neither one of us wanted to face up to the fact that he was going to die. He was going to leave me.

We went out for a drive most days and a short walk which he enjoyed, but he was so tired after he would sleep the rest of the day.

That's when I poured myself the first glass of wine or the first glass of vodka and lemonade. My crutch. My coping mechanism. Although allowing the alcohol to dull my senses, I never drank to oblivion. I still had to care for Jeff and make sure he tried to eat something before helping him to bed.

Jeff had always been close to his mum. Margaret was ninety-three and quite infirm. Before Jeff's health really started to deteriorate, he would drive up to see her every Friday, about an hour away, and take her out for lunch. He would be absolutely exhausted on his return but would not tell his mum how poorly he was.

He also continued with his voluntary work at Oxfam. I would drop him down to the shop and pick him up a few hours later.

However, Margaret's own health took a turn for the worse and she was taken into hospital where we were told she would not recover, and they could only make her comfortable.

Jeff continued to visit despite becoming weaker by the day. The one day he was too poorly to visit she passed away. His sister Sara messaged me and I broke the news to him. He was devastated he had not been with her during her final moments.

Margaret had always asked that Jeff be the one to say a few words at her service and he was determined to do that. Watching him struggle to walk to the front and say a few words set me off, and watching my children cry for their dad was heart breaking.

Life went on with several visits to the hospital by car and some by ambulance as Jeff deteriorated. Our son Tom, who lived five minutes away, always went with him.

On one occasion Jeff was put into a ward to monitor his blood pressure and a lady doctor told us in no uncertain terms that all they could do was to try a blood transfusion.

Suddenly there was a commotion in the bed next to Jeff which had curtains drawn around. I could hear shouting and swearing coming from what sounded like a very drunk man. He was shouting at a nurse that he didn't want his f---ing face stitched up and two security guards were holding him down.

I looked at my poor dear husband who had been a police superintendent and a very proud man, and then through a gap in the curtain at a drunken idiot who was trying to hit a nurse for trying to help him! What a difference.

I could feel my blood boiling and started towards the curtain, but Tom in a very calm voice said, "Don't, Mum." Which is exactly what his dad would have said.

I did ask one of the security guards to move him as it was upsetting my family, and luckily they obliged. I could hear the drunken idiot shouting all the way down the ward.

Luckily, after a blood transfusion I was able to bring Jeff home again the next day. I did not know that it would be for the last time.

A very small part of me kept thinking he was going to beat this. There was no way I was going to lose him. We were a team. I had to make him better!

My sixtieth birthday was looming and my father's ninetieth and we had planned to do something special for both, but it was looking doubtful.

So, the night of 1st July 2020 I made Jeff comfortable for the night, but as soon I made my way downstairs he shouted for me. I could see he was very distressed and wanted to go to the bathroom. I helped him get there and then rang Tom. I also rang an ambulance. But I was to regret that decision later.

Tom arrived and went into the bathroom to help his dad use the toilet, but suddenly the room was awash with blood and poo. It was explosive and went into the bath, on the walls and floor.

I rang for an ambulance again screaming for help. The ambulance took an hour to arrive and then two turned up. While we waited Jeff bled again and again, and Tom and I couldn't clear it up fast enough. It was horrendous!

Eventually, the ambulance left with Jeff with Tom riding along with him. I rang my daughter Robyn who lived near Derriford Hospital at the time and she said she would meet us there. A very kind neighbour helped me clear up and then drove me into Derriford.

I saw Robyn standing outside the casualty department but no ambulance! We went into the department to enquire where the ambulance was and we were told it was on its way – eta fifteen minutes! What the hell? It had left twenty minutes before me. Eventually, it arrived and I could see by the look on Tom's face that something had happened. Apparently, the ambulance had turned right out of our street and Tom only realised it wasn't going in the right direction when he saw the radio mast at Princetown, the opposite way to Plymouth where the hospital is. So, they turn around and then back through Tavistock but then turn into a little village called Horrabridge. Tom told them again they were not going the right way and offered to navigate but was told to calm down.

Jeff was trolleyed in and given a blood transfusion which gave him a little colour back, but he was very poorly and vomited blood all over the place. It was so distressing we kept taking it in turns to go outside. Jeff was eventually given a bed in the MAU department which is probably the busiest ward in the hospital.

We left to go home around 1am for a few hours' sleep and that's all we got as at 7am the phone rang.

Chapter Two –
My proud husband

Jeff had joined the police service at the age of sixteen going in as a cadet. He went out to Addis Ababa to work in a school for a year teaching the Duke of Edinburgh award scheme. The police did this annually to various countries, but Jeff was the last cadet to go as the young cadet following him was bitten by a tsetse fly and died.

Jeff then joined the real police at the age of eighteen. He soon become sergeant and then detective inspector at Launceston police station. This is where he met me. I was on the drug squad at the time. I had met Jeff before when he was a sergeant and going undercover in a local festival which was renowned for drug dealing. He wanted to know what sort of drugs he should be looking out for. He was dressed in tatty jeans and a waistcoat. He was unshaven and after ten minutes he had stunk my office out!

However, when I went to meet my new inspector, a few months later, I fell in love. A few months after that we were married, and I was moved to Plymouth as husbands could not be your bosses!

In time Jeff progressed to the rank of chief inspector and then superintendent. Not bad for a council house lad.

We lived in Tavistock and by the time Jeff started moving up the ranks I left the police force and had our first child in 1989 who we named Thomas David Frederick Hammond.

Three years later we had our second child, a daughter, who we named Robyn Alexandra Casson Hammond.

I was relatively healthy then and although I liked the odd night out and parties, would not have considered myself a heavy drinker. With two young children to care for and a husband who worked very long hours it was not possible.

Jeff was a fitness fanatic who would run, cycle, walk and row. Rowing was his passion and during the summer months he would go out rowing several times a week.

He was a quietly spoken man and made little small talk, but when he did speak he had the knack of captivating his audience.

Having young children it was easier to entertain at home, and after a few red wines he could relate some very funny stories which would have people in hysterics.

He was also a very cautious man, especially involving money and would quietly scold me on several occasions about my spending. In fairness, it was usually to spoil the kids.

I loved the dinner parties. The kids were in bed and I could relax with a few glasses of wine. I only stopped when I had cleared up and fell into bed.

This was not a daily or even weekly occurrence, and I had no doubts or worries about drinking at this time. I could take it or leave it and considered myself a social drinker. I was never one to have a glass of wine on my own.

Jeff loved history and travelling. As a family we had some lovely holidays and Jeff loved travelling. The kids always came with us and enjoyed our adventures. He was so knowledgeable in history that wherever we went he had stories of old to tell the children.

He retired from the police force at the young age of fifty, having done his thirty years.

He was a loving father and latterly a doting grandad to Tom's two children, Josh and Poppy.

He loved his job as a volunteer with Oxfam and took his role as online pricer very seriously. He continued to row with his club, the Mayflower Offshore Rowing Club, and even competed in the world offshore rowing championship in Geneva at the grand old age of seventy. Not bad for an old fart, he'd say.

When my father rang to tell us he could no longer live in Cyprus, Jeff started looking around for suitable rented properties. He had always got on well with my father but wouldn't take any nonsense from him. My father was a very self-opinionated man who would never admit he was wrong. He was very demanding of me as his daughter, and Jeff knew that the move would be very stressful for me.

We found a lovely two-bed apartment overlooking the River Tavy in Tavistock. It was near the shops with level access. We thought it would be perfect for him. We didn't know quite how immobile he had become. He was a drain on us from the moment he landed at Bristol airport and was taken off the plane in a wheelchair, stinking of whisky.

Jeff dealt with Father daily. The biggest issue was his drinking. He would get so drunk he would fall. Then he couldn't get up. Down Jeff would go and pick him up and make sure he was safe in bed.

This went on for a long time. Taking him to hospital for appointments, doctor, dentist, shopping and out for a pub lunch. It was never ending, and I could see the strain it was putting on Jeff.

I would clean the apartment every Sunday and Father would often come up for Sunday lunch.

Father drank daily and refused to stop, even though we were constantly clearing up after him.

I would have thought that would put me off drinking, but it didn't. The only thing it did was to make me hate the smell of whisky even more than I had as a child.

Jeff continued caring for Father because he knew how stressful it would be for me and he wanted to save me from that. Even when he began to feel unwell, he still cared for Father. That was the sort of man he was.

Chapter Three – Passing

I drove down and picked Tom up and we made our way into Derriford Hospital where we met up with Robyn.

Jeff was still in the MAU ward which was absolutely packed. Every bed of the eight-bed ward was taken and there were quite a few visitors as well. What with the nurses and doctors we could hardly fit in.

A nurse told us on arrival that he was bleeding heavily and confirmed he was dying.

I looked at my lovely husband and saw a skeletal version of him. He was so pale he was almost transparent. I kissed him on the head and he opened his eyes and smiled. He was able to speak in a whisper and he told us what a lovely life he'd had and how proud he was of us all. He asked that his friend Ray did his eulogy and he wanted a church service and then cremation. He asked that no other family member come and see him.

We held his hand as best we could as there were only two seats and not much room. I asked three times for a private room only to be told there wasn't one.

We also kept having to leave while they mopped up all the blood that was pouring out of him, and the stench was horrific.

For a very proud man he did not deserve this indignity. I begged for a private room or quieter ward but was told there weren't any available.

On our last return to the ward, and to my amazement, lunch was being served. Those poor patients had to try and eat lunch with the awful stench that was coming from my husband. We pulled the curtain around us again and we all held his hand. He was no longer talking and his breathing was very shallow and rattily.

I was aware of the sound of a television, of visitors talking and laughing, people on their mobiles having conversations, and nurses and doctors talking.

I just wanted it to end. I wanted to scream and shout and run. To get away from that horrible place. I looked at my lovely husband and whispered, "It's time. Stop breathing, just stop breathing."

Five minutes later he took his last gasp and his chest fell flat. He was gone. My darling, darling husband had left me and the children forever.

I heard someone say, "He's passing." I opened the curtains slightly and a dear old man in the opposite bed was crying. In fact, the whole ward went quiet for a minute.

What a horrible word. "Passing". In a dictionary it means: Transient, short-lived or fleeting. Jeff was none of these!

I asked my children to get me out. We were then given a private room in which to grieve and a booklet on what to do after a bereavement. We were asked if we wanted to see him again "after they'd cleaned him up" and we said no.

How I drove home I really don't know. Robyn's boyfriend came and drove her out to my house and Tom's wife Jess also came and joined us. It was a sad bunch of people all bottling up their own emotions. We all had calls to make to family and friends which was hard, but we got them done. A lot of alcohol was consumed that day.

I thought back over the last twenty-four hours and wished and wished I had never called for an ambulance. I had his oral morphine at home. I could have looked after him and cleaned him up. He would have been so much more comfortable at home. It was something I was going to beat myself up about for a long time.

I don't know how much I drank that night. I drank myself into oblivion. I was so tired and I just wanted to sleep and make the pain go away. I slept fitfully with horrendous nightmares, and when I did wake up I felt just as tired and groggy as when I had gone to bed. At one point I didn't want to wake up, I just wanted the pain to go away.

I dragged myself up as I had work to do. I had no time to grieve. I had to register the death. I had to get a death certificate which meant returning to the hospital. I had a funeral to arrange. I had to inform various agencies that Jeff had passed away. It was all too much. I would never cope with it all. Unless of course I had a drink. I thought that might get me through it all.

Chapter Four –
The battle

According to the bereavement booklet I had been given, I had to give the bereavement team a call to request the death certificate. I was informed that the duty doctor who had witnessed the death had to be the one to sign the certificate. I also rang a local funeral director. They were brilliant and took some of the burden off me. They contacted the local vicar and we booked in a date of about two weeks for the church service and the crematorium was also booked.

The sympathy cards started to arrive and became overwhelming. Also, flowers came almost daily. In a couple of days my house looked like a florist shop!

I rang the bereavement team after a couple of days and asked when I could come in to collect the death certificate so I could register his death and proceed with the funeral arrangements. This was on top of people calling me almost nonstop. Robyn and my sister-in-law Sara were my rocks and helped support me as much as they could.

The bereavement team informed me that the doctor had not yet signed the death certificate.

The funeral directors could not collect Jeff until this was done. So, he was stuck in hospital.

I picked out his clothes that I wanted him dressed in and took them to the funeral directors. I chose his police constable's uniform as I couldn't bear to part with his superintendent's jacket as it had his long service medal on it, and he was so proud when he first wore it. He loved the police force and worked so hard to attain the rank he did.

I did give the directors one of his superintendent's caps to place on top of the coffin, and the police liaison officer contacted me to ask if I would like a Devon and Cornwall Constabulary flag to be draped over the coffin. I could picture how emotional that would be but thought Jeff would have liked that.

So, four days after his death I rang again requesting the death certificate, only to be told the doctor hadn't signed it yet!

This became a daily occurrence for ten days until I could take no more. The funeral date was looming. The announcement had gone out in the local newspaper and people were travelling from as far as Australia!

I even rang the ward where he had died to try and get some help. The funeral directors also rang to explain the situation but to no avail.

Two days before the funeral I thought I was going to have a breakdown. I had decided to do the eulogy myself as no one knew Jeff better than me. His rowing buddy Ray was also going to do one and Robyn was going to read a poem with Tom standing next to her in support.

But there was no Jeff. He was still stuck in the damn hospital because no one could bother to chase the doctor to sign the certificate.

Simon, the funeral director, rang me late afternoon with two days to go and said he had never experienced this before, and we may have to go ahead with the service without Jeff.

I had an absolute meltdown. I cried and screamed and drank! I rang again and was told the doctor in question was on duty and they would ask her to sign it. At last!

Simon rang me at 5pm and said they still hadn't released the body to them.

I didn't know what else to do. I was at my wits end. How could we possibly have a funeral without Jeff?

I then remembered one of the letters I had received, stating if there was anything he could do to help me and my family please contact him. The writer of this letter was the chief constable of Devon and Cornwall Constabulary.

I rang Simon back and asked him to ring the hospital again and tell them the chief constable would be ringing the CEO of the hospital asking why ex-Superintendent Hammond's body is not being released to his family

Two hours later Simon rang to say he was on his way back from hospital with Jeff.

The following day, one day before the funeral, my sister-in-law Sara and Tom and Robyn and I went to the funeral parlour to say our last goodbyes.

The chapel was small and we all squeezed in. Jeff was lying in an open coffin wearing his police uniform. He looked so tiny compared to the stocky man he had been. I touched his face and hand and felt the coldness. I just wanted to warm him up. We all said a few words and just wept. It wasn't too long before I wanted to leave. I badly needed a drink.

The following day just before 11am the hearse arrived outside my house with a limo behind for close family. Tom had already gone down as he was one of the pallbearers.

The pall bearers were Tom and James Burns, Mike and Harry Moss, and Oliver and Frazer Clark.
My brother I needed with me.
I looked at the coffin draped with the Devon and Cornwall Constabulary flag and his superintendent's hat on top. I broke down and sobbed my heart out. How the hell was I going to get through this day? I had the eulogy to do. The vicar had kindly asked me for a copy of the eulogy so he could take over if I broke down and couldn't continue. There was no way that was going to happen! I owed it to Jeff to finish. I had read it and read it so many times and each time the crying became less. I had read it so many times I had taken the emotion out of it.

I did have to ask the vicar if I was permitted to say one thing in a church. Both our children broke stuff from time to time as did Josh. No one ever thought it was a problem as Jeff was so clever he could fix virtually anything. We had a saying in our house and a plaque on the entrance wall: "If Grandad can't fix it, we're screwed".

The vicar laughed at that and reassured me that was fine.

I knew there would probably be a fair few at the church, but when the vicar came out and announced there were around three hundred I started to shake. Not the time to have a panic attack.

I lifted my head high and walked in with my family following the coffin and the six pallbearers.

My father was already there at the front and had parked himself in the aisle sat on his wheelchair.

The service was lovely and I managed to start my eulogy. Once I started I was fine, and because it was about Jeff's life there were a few funny anecdotes where people laughed. At the end I went to step down but heard the whole church clapping. I looked at the vicar as I wasn't sure that was appropriate but I could see him clapping too.

I don't think I had ever attended a funeral where people had applauded, and it took me by surprise.

Jeff's rowing friend went next and then Robyn read out her poem beautifully with Tom standing by her side.

Josh had joined Tom when he had sat down and I glanced over to give him a smile, but he was crying so bad it set me off again.

I walked out of the church holding his hand telling him to hold his head up and be proud. I thought he had done amazing even to get there at such a young age, but he had loved his grandad and had done so much with him. All good memories.

The wake was held at the Bedford Hotel which was right opposite the church. We all piled in and there was coffee and tea prepared, but it also had a bar where people were already queuing up.

There were so many people there who wanted to speak with me I didn't have the chance to move for about an hour. Luckily, people were asking what I wanted to drink, and I already had several white wines on the go.

Food arrived but by the time I got to it most of it had gone. They had to bring a second buffet out.

Jeff had gone to the crematorium in Plymouth but I had decided not to go. My brother-in-law Mike had gone with the hearse.

I stayed to the end saying goodbye to the last person. I was exhausted. Also, slightly tipsy!

Chapter Five –
Decisions and indecisions

Friends and family visited almost on a daily rota. It was nice to have company, but it was also nice to have some time on my own to grieve.

Also, there were mundane issues to be sorted like informing all the companies who needed to be informed of Jeff's death and hiring a solicitor to sort out probate.

My father was also becoming increasingly difficult and kept ringing asking me to take him out. I didn't want to go out and didn't want to see anyone. I asked my brother to ask my father to leave me alone for a bit. I only wanted to see Robyn, Tom and his wife Jess, my two grandchildren and my brother.

Friends came and went and in time the phone calls and visits dropped off.

My sixtieth birthday was looming and I decided to take my family and go and spend a weekend at the Elfordleigh Hotel which was a golf club and spa hotel.

So, on 9th August Tom and Jess, Robyn and her boyfriend James, and Josh and Poppy all met at the hotel to try and have a fun weekend. We all hit the pool and spa and then the bar for food and drink. Lots of drink!

The following day after breakfast I returned to my room to find it all decorated and a load of presents. It was an emotional time but I tried to hold it together for the sake of everyone else's enjoyment.

The evening was spent drinking and eating, crying and laughing. Tom and Josh had gone off in a golf buggy during the afternoon, and Tom had played some golf which he had played with Jeff many years ago.

Everyone had had a busy day with quite a lot of exercise and we were all pretty whacked. A waiter kindly took a photo of me with my family around me. Tom and Jess knew but no one else did that this would probably be the last birthday of mine Tom would see.

This is the photo on the rear of the book.

I made some poor decisions and some good ones.

I spent a lot of money on the house, putting in paving slabs and a gate giving me more privacy. I think that was a good one. The poor one was choosing a friend of Tom's to do the paving. My garden looked like a bomb site for months as he just wouldn't come back and finish the job.

I bought a Kawasaki 300cc scooter which I loved, until I wrote it off injuring myself quite badly.

I bought a black lab puppy who I named Tag. He's two years old now and I love him to bits but he has caused so much damage to the house, ripping up the utility room floor, eating woodwork, shoes, and even £100 cash.

I bought an inflatable Kayak which sunk on the first trip out.

I knocked out the upstairs bathroom with a sledgehammer, as I could not get the vision of Tom holding Jeff on the toilet with blood and poo splattered everywhere out of my mind.

I sold Jeff's MGC as I could not drive it and I sold the caravan as I could not tow it.

I gave an awful lot of money away to family members to help them out.

I put the house on the market and then took it off again a month later.

I bought a trampoline and large swimming pool for the grandchildren.

I bought an electric mountain bike which I fell off three times, the last being onto a kerb and cracking some ribs.

I had the wall knocked down between the kitchen and dining room. The work is still ongoing as I am writing this, as is the amount of dust! As I said a lot of decisions. Some good. Some poor. Some made with sober clarity and some with drunken madness, thinking they were good decisions at the time. The following day I would wake up and not even remember what I had bought off Amazon until it arrived.

Chapter Six – Tom

It was a couple of weeks after my birthday and I was sitting on the lawn playing with Tag.

It was a beautiful sunny day and Tag was being funny and I remember smiling at him. There weren't many things that made me smile these days. My older dog Tess was sprawled out in the sun and kept very patient when Tag tried to pull her ears. I couldn't help but smile.

Suddenly, I saw Tom and Jess walk around the side of the house with Jess carrying Poppy. I smiled but then saw that Jess was really upset and had been crying.

Thomas David Frederick Hammond was born on 17th October 1989. I was the age of thirty and Jeff was forty-two.

At the time of our marriage we were both in the police force and very keen to make a career out of it. I was going places and nothing was going to hold me back. From the grand old age of twelve I had always loved *Z Cars* and used to watch it with my grandpa. I was enthralled with the excitement of being a police officer. "Goodnight all" at the end of the show made me feel safe and I wanted to do that.

At the age of sixteen when *Starsky and Hutch* hits the screen I was in no doubt that I wanted to be a police officer, a detective, a solver of crimes, and best of all to stop bullying which I detested and still do.

However, things didn't go as planned and I failed my sergeant's exam twice, missing out by three points on the final one.

Then, a car accident brought my career to an end and I was invalided out of the police force.

I was bored stiff for a year and drank far too much with a friend who later became a chronic alcoholic.

So, I said one evening, do you fancy having a baby? Jeff's grin and hug told me the answer.

Tom was born and he was the most perfect beautiful baby ever. I know every parent says that, but he really was. Weighing in at 9 pounds 4 ounces he was so healthy and smiled at me within hours. The nurse said it was wind but I knew he smiled. All his life that's what he did. No matter what life threw at him, he always had a smile.

Tom grew into a healthy, very active toddler, and when his little sister was born he played the big brother. There was a three year age difference, but Tom made it his mission to look after, protect and nag his little sister. As small children they were very close, but when Tom went to school he found there were others out there that wanted his company. He was a popular lad and soon made friends that would stand by him for the whole of his life.

Tom loved football but also played rugby, cricket, tennis and golf. He was the local comic, always getting up to mischief and never still. I always remember the milk challenge. A group of Tom's friends would buy a two pint carton of milk, sneak off to the top of the garden and see who could drink it the fastest without throwing up! They all thought it hilarious.

As he grew older the milk changed to beer and Tom loved going out with his mates and sinking a few beers. Jeff was in despair some nights when he hadn't come home. It was a rule to let us know if he was staying with a friend and wasn't coming home. Sometimes he would forget. Needless to say he got a rollicking when he did stagger home.

Tom was now an adult and we had to respect that he was finding his feet. He did well at school and managed to get an apprenticeship with Babcock Marine as a marine engineer. We were so proud of him. He had beaten off loads of competition.

His aim was to see out his apprenticeship and then look at joining the Royal Marines.

One night that all changed. His girlfriend Jessie was over and they had been watching TV in his bedroom. As Tom walked across the front room to join me and Jeff he suddenly stopped and stared down at the floor. It looked like he was trying to swallow but couldn't. We asked him if he was all right but he couldn't speak. Jessie said he had been having a couple of funny turns like that recently.

As a lad of nine Tom had suffered headaches which, when bad, made him vomit. We took him to the doctor time and time again and we were told the same thing. Childhood migraines and that he would grow out of them eventually.

I will never ever forgive myself for the rest of my life. If only we had not settled for that opinion. Would it have made a difference? Would it have given him a chance?

Why did Jeff and I just accept what a doctor said? Why did we never question anything?

At the age of nineteen Tom was finally called in for a scan.

The following day I can remember vividly. I was at home and Jeff was at his rowing club.

The phone went and I answered it. I was told it was a doctor from Derriford and he needed Tom in immediately. I explained he had had his scan yesterday so why did he have to come in again?

He replied it was about the scan and then refused to give me any more information, despite my pleading.

I rang Jeff and he went to the dockyard to pick Tom up. I picked Jessie up and we all met at the hospital.

We sat in the waiting room for what seemed like an eternity. People came and went and we just sat there. I think being last in should give you a hint of what was to come.

I became concerned about the ticket on my car as it was due to run out, but when the receptionist heard me talk about it she said she would ring down to the parking office and clear it with them.

That's when I knew the news wasn't going to be good.

Jeff and Tom eventually went in and Jessie and I sat there, not daring to speak. Time went by and eventually the door that I had been staring at opened and Tom came and walked off up the corridor. I could see how upset he was but I let Jessie be the one to go after him.

I went into the room where Jeff was still with the doctor and Jeff quickly explained that the scan showed a brain tumour.

After that I just remember grabbing hold of the doctor and shouting at him, "Don't you let him die, don't you dare let him die!"

Chapter Seven – So much pain

I always thought that Jeff was the bravest man I knew, but he wasn't. It was Tom. He sat on an outside seat and quietly explained that the tumour had turned nasty. He explained that it was no longer a grade two glioma – non-malignant – but an aggressive cancerous tumour that was inoperable.

Jess began to cry again and I just collapsed face down on the grass and sobbed and sobbed. No! This was just a dream. A nightmare but just a horrible dream. If I open my eyes and stop crying it will all go away.

Tom calmly told me he had no longer than fifteen months. I couldn't speak. I could hardly breathe. Not my boy. My nice kind considerate loving son. It wasn't fair. Why couldn't it be someone else? Some horrible boy who was no good to anyone!

Tom had two little children who adored him. How were we going to tell Josh?

They stayed for a bit longer and we all had a drink. After they left I had a lot more.

If I was going to end my life, it was then.

How on earth could I outlive my son who I adored? My first-born child who I unquestionably would have laid down my life for. What was the point? I felt I couldn't take any more pain. It was just too much to cope with. What did I have in the house? Vodka, morphine from Jeff, and tablets.

If I was strong enough I could do it. I sat there in the lounge with the vodka, the morphine bottle, which was half full, and about twenty paracetamols.

I wondered briefly how all that was going to make me feel. I wondered if it was going to be quick. I wondered if it was going to be painful.

I looked at my two dogs who stared at me with love and hope and I crumbled. I thought about my darling daughter and what she had been through. How could I put her through that again? Josh and Poppy had lost so much. Could they really lose a granny as well?

I also had a brother that loved me, my father to care for, and Jess and my sister-in-law Sara.

I drank the vodka but poured the morphine down the sink. The tablets I put back in the cupboard.

Yet another night of oblivion. Blanking it all out again and another hangover to wake up to.

Tom deteriorated quickly and he began to lose the use of his left arm and his face on the left was frozen. He continued smiling though, but it was rather lop-sided.

He wanted to make memories with his children and we all went out as much as we could. Jess planned a short holiday to Disneyland Paris but it wasn't to be.

Christmas came around and it was my first one without Jeff. I really wanted to be on my own and I knew it was probably going to be Tom's last.

Tom and Jess wanted to spend it at their house with Josh and Poppy. I said to Robyn that she should spend it with James, which she was reluctant to do, but accepted my wishes.

It was a beautiful sunny day and I thought I might take the dogs for a long walk around Pew Tor.

When I returned I cooked a small roast dinner, lit the fire and watched films for the rest of the day. I also drunk quite a lot of wine. Well, it was Christmas Day!

Boxing Day arrived and the family came to me for lunch. I honestly can't remember what we had but we had a good time opening presents and drinking. By the time everyone left I could hardly stand up.

New year approached and traditionally we always had Josh, ever since he was a baby. But this year his mum was having a house party and he wanted to stay with her as his friends were coming too.

I fully understood but it was weird not having him stay. I went to bed early as there was nothing to celebrate.

January dragged on and it was the first January Jeff and I didn't go to the Canaries for our winter sun holiday. I thought about it but was not inclined to go on my own.

In early October the surgeons in charge of Tom explained that the main tumour had grown very large and other tumours were growing off it. They decided he needed a debulking which would take away some of the tumour and ease the pressure on his brain. It was hoped it would lessen his seizures and give him some quality of the life he had left. By this time his left side was virtually paralysed and he could not use his left arm. He fell a lot as his left leg was also going the same way. His smile, which unbelievably he did a lot, was lop-sided as the left side of his face was also paralysed.

On the day of the operation I picked Jess and Tom up and met up with Robyn at the hospital shortly after 7am.

The queue to the ward was ridiculous and we had to wait in line for twenty minutes with no seats to sit on. Poor Tom was really struggling, but he refused to go past the queue to sit down while we checked him in.

The operation was going to be done with Tom awake, the reason being he could be in constant communication with the anaesthetist. This was mainly so he could say if he was getting feeling back or losing more feeling in his body. Tom wasn't fazed by this at all. I was scared stiff. I just didn't want him in any more pain. Little did we know after waiting seven very long boring hours that it wasn't going to happen that way after all.

Chapter Eight – Alternative health

When Tom had the diagnosis of being inoperable and terminal, Jess began looking at alternative medicine. We both researched it and a friend of mine, Caroline, invited me and Tom to her house. She had also been diagnosed with terminal cancer and she had gone down the alternative route as well as the traditional one. She advised lots of alternative medicine but I could see Tom was sceptical.

The main ones we picked up on were Panacur dog worming tablets and CBC oil. Tom agreed to give it a go. Both were expensive, and a friend started a GoFundMe page on Facebook. In total it raised more than £20,000.

Panacur was government monitored and you had to put in the dog's details to receive it. I thought it was odd at the time but ordered some as did a load of his friends, making up dogs' names just to get the stuff.

We realised CBC oil wasn't strong enough and Jess managed to get hold of a dealer who would supply THC (the illegal stuff) and very strong. Also, very expensive.

Tom was soon taking a lot of alternative medicine and was pretty bombed out most of the time, but apart from sleeping a lot he had a huge appetite. Jess put him on a strict keto diet which was also supposed to be a cancer fighter, but Tom had such a sweet tooth she would often find him woofing down Poppy's little sugary snacks!

Tom remained content and happy to be at home with a lot of friends visiting and helping with Poppy. There were so many I could not name them all, but they were damn good friends. Friends can be defined as supporters and helpers. They were most definitely that. They would do anything for Tom or Jess, what you would call true friends.

As a family we managed a few roast dinners, sometimes at mine, sometimes at a local pub. Tom loved roast potatoes but he was not supposed to have them on his keto diet. He would always look at Jess and ask if he could just have a few. Jess always said yes and he would tuck into them, eating more than a few and washed down with a few beers.

He would smile at me as if he had won a major battle. Tom would do anything for his wife, who he loved passionately. They were both so good-looking with a real zest for life and were the perfect couple. Jess took on Tom knowing he had a brain tumour and little Josh from a previous relationship. A lot for such a young girl but she did it without any misgivings. She loved Tom with all her heart so she accepted that their time together may be short.

Jess became a loving stepmother to Josh and Josh's mum Jessie became close friends.

Josh adored Poppy and she remains his only little sister as his mum went on to have two more boys. They have a special relationship, and when Poppy sees Josh her whole face lights up.

Chapter Nine –
The operation

After waiting for several hours in Derriford Hospital, I politely asked the receptionist how much longer we would have to wait as Tom was really struggling to stay awake on a very uncomfortable seat.

She said she didn't know. I asked her if she could ring someone and she said she didn't think there were any beds available and that was the delay. People had been going in and out all day. Why was Tom the last?

She offered a trolley so he could lay down. Tom declined.

Ten minutes later the surgeon came to see us and apologised for the wait. He could see by my face that I wasn't happy.

He also explained that the procedure would now been done by general anaesthetic as the anaesthetist had been called to another case. He said it wasn't ideal but he had no other choice. Before I could reply Tom agreed that it was fine. It wasn't bloody fine at all! Tom was having to undergo a complicated operation in not the best way. They could muck it up and he could die. Was it just me? I looked at everyone else and they seemed so calm.

We walked Tom down to the operating theatre and we all gave him a kiss goodbye. He turned around and grinned. He had such a lovely smile.

We all went home. Jess to cry. Robyn to be angry. Me to drink.

The following day we heard that Tom had survived the operation and was in a ward for serious head trauma. We all took it in turns to visit so we could still administer his alternative medicine. Poor Tom, after we gave him his

THC he was high as a kite. I think the nurses were suspicious, as you could smell the cannabis THC oil as soon as you walked in the ward.

In the end Jess decided he was on so many different painkillers that he should stop the alternative for the time being. It was making him sleep practically all day and night.

Josh visited and when they saw each other Josh burst into tears. He cried again when it was time to leave, and I knew he was afraid that every visit might be his last. Poppy also visited her daddy and would climb up on his bed for cuddles. The ward had a real mixed bunch of people, with an elderly man completely paralysed and a young lad who had serious brain trauma having been hit by a drunk driver. I can only take my hat off to the nurses working on such a difficult ward.

Tom had half of his head shaved and the scar was horrendous. Jess tried to get some information about the operation but always got the same reply: "It went as well as it could!"

Tom's seizures improved so I guess in that way it was a success and would give him the time he had left to make memories with his children.

Robyn came up with the idea of having a fundraiser for Tom in the hope they would be able to have a little family holiday.

She amazed me with her organisational skills, and it wasn't long before she had booked a date at the local rugby club, booked the food, the music and an auction.

The generosity of the Tavistock people was amazing and soon my office was full of stuff to be raffled. So many businesses donated things like free MOTs, free dinners in a top restaurant, beauty therapy, paintings and signed football and rugby shirts. We also had smaller stuff for a raffle.

One of Robyn's friends, Sky Scott, announced that if the GoFundMe page reached £20,000 she would have her head shaved at the rugby club and donate it to make wigs for women who had lost theirs through chemotherapy. It didn't look like it was going to reach the target, but the day before the fundraiser it suddenly soared up to the £20,000 mark.

Tom would still be in hospital on the day, but he knew it was happening. He was overwhelmed with everyone's generosity, and I knew he would have loved to come and have a few beers with his mates.

Chapter Ten –
The fundraiser

The date soon came and my brother Hugh came up to stay with me for the weekend. He was my big brother but I always seemed to be helping him out with various issues. Now he was there for me, which I found strange, but I needed him so bad. He was an absolute rock when I needed him most.

We went up early with Jess and her best friend Taz coming later, as they wanted to fit in a visit to Tom.

We decorated and set up all the raffle and auction items. The singer set up in the corner and everything was going to plan. I'd had a few wines before we went up there, and as we were sorting everything I had a few more. Luckily, Hugh doesn't drink much so I knew he would get me home.

Robyn was drinking a fair bit as well but I knew her boyfriend, James, would make sure she was okay.

So many people arrived and the evening soon got underway. The lady who had donated her hair was soon shaven and cried, bless her, which set me off. Josh who was there with his mum thought it was hilarious and went around to pick it all up.

A lot of people were drinking that night so I didn't feel guilty. This was a special day after all, a special day to fundraise for a special family who were loved by so many people that it was almost overwhelming.

The singer was amazing and soon everyone was getting up to dance or grab something to eat, all food having been donated and cooked on the premises. Everyone knew Tom and I felt humbled in the effort people had made to come here and all the funny stories they had and the memories of their escapades, some of which I hadn't known which was probably for the best.

Tom was a popular local lad loved by many and disliked by none. I can never remember anyone ever saying a bad word about him.

As the night wore on the auction started and people gave the most amazing bids for items. The amount of cash and pledges were awe-inspiring! Thank goodness I had friends who could keep a tally, as I was passed it. I knew I should have had something to eat.

But where was Jess? I suddenly realised she wasn't here. I tried ringing her but it went straight to voicemail. I rang and rang as did Robyn but no reply. Now I was worried about her. Had she had an accident driving back from Plymouth? OMG, what else was going to happen?

Suddenly, the male singer who was doing the raffle stopped. The next words that came out of his mouth absolutely floored me.

"Ladies and gentlemen and kids. I have just had the word that TOM HAMMOND IS ENTERING THE BUILDING."

Everything just stopped. Time stopped. My heart stopped. I looked at the door and saw my son coming in slowly holding on to a walker, with Jess and Taz beaming either side of him.

I didn't know that Jess had been asking the hospital all day if they could take Tom out for a couple of hours. They didn't ring back till they were just about to come up to the rugby club, so they went shooting in to get him. The lad who had had the accident begged to come as well, bless him, but he wasn't allowed.

As Tom walked in Robyn, Josh and I went running over to him. To say I was sobbing was an understatement. Josh was crying, Robyn was crying, and we just went into a group hug. Everyone else was in shock too but respectfully kept their distance. It seemed like a time without end. I never wanted to move ever again. Jess joined us and we all just hugged and cried. Except Tom of course, he wanted us all to stop crying. Hugh later said that he had been through a lot but had never witnessed anything so emotional in his life. In fact, a lot of people said that.

As we pulled away Tom went to sit down and his mates came over, just a few at a time to have a chat and spend some time with him. Everyone was amazed that he had made it and it was truly the icing on the cake.

I don't remember much else. I just couldn't stop crying and asked Hugh to take me home. I kissed and hugged Tom and said that I would see him tomorrow in the hospital. His reply? "Mum, you don't have to come in every day. I know Derriford has bad memories because of Dad."

That was my son. Always thinking about others.

Chapter Eleven –
Tom's thirtieth birthday

Not long after the fundraiser Tom was allowed to come home. His thirtieth birthday was looming and nobody really knew what to do. He was still very poorly and we all knew we wanted to do something but didn't know what.

In the end Jess, Robyn and I agreed we should throw him a surprise party at mine. Just a few close friends.

I decorated the house with loads of banners and balloons with 30 on them. Jess had organised the cake and dropped it round in the morning. The food was booked with Blue Sky catering and being an old friend she hardly charged me anything. I, of course, bought loads of alcohol but everyone brought something.

Everything was set and one friend turned up all the way from Scotland. I guess there were about thirty invited as there were always some who couldn't make it. Everyone turned up and arrived early, parking in the road away from my house.

The plan was that Jess was going to tell Tom she had booked a quiet meal out but was popping in to see me on the way.

She messaged me giving me a five-minute warning. Everyone hid behind the lounge/dining room wall.

I could hardly contain myself. The food was set up, the decorations up and there was plenty of alcohol.

I opened the door and saw Tom's smiling face, albeit a bit lop-sided. He gave me a huge hug and said what he said every time he saw me. "All right, Mum?"

I told them to go in the lounge and I would get them a drink. But I followed them in. Suddenly everyone jumped out and said, "Surprise!"

I looked at Tom's shocked face and he looked horrified. Oh no. What had I done? Perhaps he did want a quiet meal out with Jess. Why did I always interfere?

Then he smiled at everyone and everyone came out and gave him a hug. He sat on the sofa and everyone came over and chatted with him. Drink flowed, the food got eaten and the music level went up.

I don't think anyone realised that would be the last birthday he would ever have.

After everyone had left I started to clear up, but I had drunk so much and became so tearful I ended up just going to bed. I could clear up in the morning.

The following morning I came down to utter chaos. My first duty however was to walk the dogs. That done I began to clear up the mess. It must have taken me the best part of the day. Getting all the decorations down probably took the longest. The food that was left I either ate or binned and the alcohol left I probably drank.

Jess messaged me to say what a lovely evening it had been and Tom had really enjoyed it. That made everything worth the effort and mess. My boy had had a nice evening.

Apart from his paralysis in his left arm and leg and the left side of his face, he had been happy and laughing and even trying to dance!

He was a fighter and so brave. There was no way this was going to beat him. There was a cure out there and we would find it. I could not lose my first-born child. It was unthinkable and I could not get my head around that it might happen. Okay, so block it out every night with alcohol. So much easier to deal with then.

Chapter Twelve – The last Christmas

For the first time ever Tom and Jess wanted to spend Christmas in their own house. Usually they came to me or Jess's mum. We alternated with either having them Christmas Day or Boxing Day. So, in that way they could enjoy two roast dinners.

This year they wanted to have theirs at home along with Poppy and Josh.

I had no issues with that at all and wanted to spend Christmas on my own.

They did invite me down but I declined. I said I would pop down in the morning for a bit but woke up with such a bad stomach I messaged them to say I couldn't make it.

After a long dog walk, I lit the fire and showered and put my PJs on. I sat in front of the TV and opened my first bottle of wine. I started to feel better and as the evening wore on it felt cosy and right.

I made myself a small roast dinner and then started the prep work for Boxing Day when all the family was coming to me.

On Boxing Day I honestly don't remember what we ate, but we played silly games and had a quiz. Of course, alcohol was involved and we all got quite merry.

We swapped presents and it was a lovely family day. A family that was going to be cut to pieces – again.

Poor Jeff. He never knew what to get me for a present. Not my birthday or Christmas. Anniversaries were always flowers as was Valentine's day.

He was always so concerned about getting it right but never did. I asked him to never buy me clothes but he always did and always got the size wrong, so they were either too baggy or too tight.

I think the worst birthday present ever was a Slendertone belt, a kitchen radio and a steam iron. I don't think I spoke to him for a week!

At least this Christmas my lovely dear husband didn't have that worry. How I would love for him to have given me some too tight tops or another steam iron just for him to be there with me.

Although, to be honest, the news of Tom would probably have finished him off. They had such a loving close relationship and were always there for each other. When Tom came up to our house they always shook hands and hugged. They did the same when Tom left.

They saw each other at least once a week so it wasn't like a quick visit after several months. We were a close family.

Waiting for the beautiful bride. Robyn, Josh, me and Jeff

Jess and Tom on their wedding day

Wedding day. Tom and Jeff always having a laugh

Jess and Tom on their wedding day

The birth of Poppy with Tom, Robyn and Josh

Tom resting at home with his family on an orthopaedic bed set up in their front room

Poppy visiting Daddy at St. Lukes during covid lockdown

Chapter Thirteen –
Tom's wedding day

When Tom rang to say he had proposed to Jess I cried. I turned to Jeff and said, "He's done it. Finally. He's proposed to Jess."

Jeff just smiled and said, "I know, I had to help him out with the ring."

I couldn't believe it! He had kept a secret from me! But it was a nice one.

So, the wedding plans began and to be honest I don't think Tom had a lot to do with it. Jess organised everything. They booked the venue and all the accommodation. Trevenna was between Liskeard and Bodmin and it was the perfect setting.

We went down for a taster session to choose the menu and it was wonderful. I was driving so didn't get to sample the wine. Everyone else got a little tipsy. There was one thing I would never do and still don't to this day, and that's drink and drive. I would rather have nothing than just one glass of wine. One glass leads to another and another.

On Friday 22nd September 2018 we all headed off to the venue. Jeff had made some posts with signs directing people in so they had to be put out first.

On the Friday evening most of the family were meeting up at the venue. Jess's father and stepmum, Helen, had come over from Spain as had her brother Dan. The other three half-brothers also arrived as had her mum Kay and stepdad Stan.

We had a lovely evening together and a lovely meal, but not wanting to feel ill on the big day I had an early night.

The chalets were amazing and we shared ours with Robyn and James. On the wedding night Josh was coming in with us but that night he spent with his dad.

Josh was one of the pageboys and he was so excited.

The venue was decorated mostly by Jess, and although she had helpers she knew exactly what she wanted. She had literally thought of everything, even down to the Jager Bombs after the toast and the cupcakes. The wedding cake was beautiful. It was almost too good to cut.

My father couldn't make the wedding as he still lived in Cyprus at the time, but my brother and nephews did as well as my sister-in-law Sara and her husband Mike. A carer brought down my mum-in-law as she did not want to stay over.

The weather had been awful with storms and high winds, but on the day of the wedding it brightened up and we were told we could have it outside rather than in. The aisle was swept of leaves and the seats all put out.

I did happen to notice that a lot of people had started drinking in the morning, when the wedding wasn't until 2pm. I didn't as I knew I would have to pace myself. Once I started that was it!

I watched Tom sink pint after pint and became a little concerned. Suddenly, everyone realised that time was going on and we all needed to get ready. I had a frock to wear for the ceremony. Anyone who knows me knows I hate frocks!

I even had my hair done from one of the hairdressers Jess had brought in.

What I didn't notice was that Jess wasn't drinking. I was to find out why later.

So, we all walked down to where it had all been set up. All the chairs had been laid out and the flowers decorated the arch behind the registrar.

She was a lovely bubbly woman who immediately put Tom at ease. Tom stood next to his two best men, Rob and Jim.

A few minutes went by and I couldn't wait to see Jess in her dress. I knew she would look beautiful. Josh was one of the pageboys and the ring bearer.

I then saw Tom whisper something to the registrar and I heard her say, "Why didn't you go before you came down here?"

I laughed and said out loud, "I was going to tell him that!"

Tom started up to his chalet and the registrar, "Well run then!"

Everyone laughed. Tom just made it back in time before Jess came out with her dad holding her arm and her mum leading the procession. I was right, she looked beautiful. I looked at Tom and I could see how happy he was. He just had a huge grin on his face.

I promised myself I wouldn't, but I did. My eyes filled with tears and before I knew it tears were streaming down my face. Jeff held my hand and smiled at me. I was so proud of Tom. I think when he looked at Jess he was the happiest man on the planet at that time. He adored her, as we all did.

Jess bolted into our lives as "all right, Mum, this is Jess."

I knew he had a girl. I used to go down once a week and hoover, dust and clean his house. One day I went down and came back and said to Jeff, "Tom's got a girlfriend."

Jeff said, "How do you know that?"

I said, "Because his house is spotless!"

Jeff and I adored her from day one. She was bubbly, funny and chatty. She fitted into our family straightaway and Robyn also gave her approval.

At this present day they are the best of friends as sister-in-laws should be.

Going back to the wedding everything was perfect, apart from the best men's speech maybe.

Jess had thought of everything, down to funny photographs, to the entertainment, including all the children.

As the day wore on a lot of the evening guests started to arrive, and even more food came out.

It was such a lovely evening and I got to dance with Tom on a slow smoochy one. He wasn't embarrassed and neither was I. Yes, we were both slightly drunk, but we loved each other and it felt right.

I left early as I had Josh in with me for the night and the poor little chap was exhausted.

Tom and Jess went to Bali for their honeymoon, and apart from Tom getting bitten by a monkey they had a fabulous time.

When they returned and came up to see us they were full of the honeymoon stories. Automatically I got Tom a beer and Jess a gin and tonic. When Jess declined I knew then she was pregnant. Jess never refused a G and T.

On 19th April 2018 little Poppy Ella Hammond was born premature and weighed only 4 pounds 14 ounces. She was put in an incubator and fed only by a drip.

Tom was the proudest dad ever. He was content. He had a lovely little son, aged seven years, and now a lovely, perfect, but very little girl.

She was soon to make up for her size with a very strong personality.

Chapter Fourteen – Downfall

On Friday 17th January 2020, Tom was rushed into hospital when he became unresponsive at home.

He was sleeping a lot and after his normal afternoon nap Jess couldn't wake him.

Jess, Robyn and I sat together in the hospital ward watching Tom have seizure after seizure and then vomiting. It was just horrible and there was nothing we could do but hold his hand. I have never felt so useless as a mother. Why did it have to be Tom?

What had we as a family done to deserve this?

We had always been respectful and kind to people and Tom was so popular with his friends, our friends, and friends' children. Everyone loved Tom. He was funny, did daft things, but made everyone laugh.

He lived life to the full. One of his tattoos was "Love the life you live. Live the life you love".

He loved going with Jess and their friends to Creamfields where they would take a two-man tent and wellies and a few beers and enjoy the music, the mayhem and the friendship.

He was so full of life and vigour. How was he now lying in a hospital bed dying in front of us?

A female doctor took us aside and explained he had had a bleed on the brain and was not likely survive it. She further explained that it was very common for a person to have another bigger one and suffer heart failure. She asked us if we wanted resuscitation.

I remember looking at Jess as everything had to be her decision, but I was screaming inside. Please don't let him die. I would never be ready to accept my son was dying before me.

As I choked back the tears, I decided. I had watched my darling husband take his last breaths, I was not about to do the same with my son. How unsupportive and lame was that.

I apologised and told Robyn and Jess I was leaving. I just couldn't do it.

The amount of visitors Tom had was phenomenal. There were groups of them sat all over the hospital, taking it in turns to sit with Tom, help him to the toilet and hold his hand during his seizures.

Jess and her mum camped out and slept wherever they could find room, as did one of Tom's best mates Jamie Doyle.

Tom stayed with us and on 23rd January was moved to St. Luke's hospice at Plymstock. It was further to go but what a lovely place with lovely staff. We all knew that if you went into a hospice you didn't normally come out.

Tom was to prove us wrong yet again. He was not going to give up one moment of being with his family.

Chapter Fifteen – St Luke's Hospice

On my first visit I found Tom and Jess in a lovely big light room with a bed big enough for both.

Tom said his seizures had improved, and although still tired was not in too much pain. He said he could have more pain relief if he wanted it but it knocked him out, so he didn't want to take too much.

Tom's appetite was huge and he tucked into three meals a day, which a restaurant would have been proud to serve.

He was even allowed a rum and Coke late morning before his three-course meal.

If he wasn't so poorly it would have been like staying in a five-star hotel.

There was no restriction on visitors and soon his friends came and went and left time for family only visits.

Josh came to visit and was able to go on a PlayStation with Tom, have lunch together and go for a short walk outside. It had been explained to Josh that Daddy was in a special hospital and that was where he would stay. He was told he wouldn't be coming home.

We had been told that the bleed on the brain could happen again, and the next time could cause a stroke.

However, we were also told that in rare cases the brain could reabsorb the blood and recover.

I visited every day taking the dogs with me as I was able to walk them in a field opposite the hospice. It just meant I could stay longer and enjoy a very nice lunch in the café.

There were so many of us one day that we practically took over the whole café.

I couldn't help but think Tom looked quite well. I knew not to get my hopes up, but a small part of me wouldn't let go in believing he could still beat this.

I just wasn't ready to lose him. I knew I would never be.

A week later Jess had popped home to catch up with Poppy and get some clean clothes, and I arranged to meet my friend Sharon at the hospice.

As we walked in Tom smiled. He asked if Jess was coming to fetch him. I didn't take on board what he was saying until he smiled again and said, "I can go home." Oh boy did I cry.

There was no point Jess coming all the way in, so I rang her to say I was bringing Tom home. Inevitably she cried as well. For once though, they were happy tears.

Tom had also been told he was strong enough to take more chemotherapy, a new kind and a very strong one.

Once again there was a little bit of hope.

Josh of course was over the moon but also confused as he had been told Daddy wasn't coming home.

Once again Tom had beaten the odds!

That weekend we managed a fun morning at a park with Josh and Poppy and then met Robyn and James and his grandparents at a pub just outside Plymouth. Tom enjoyed a hearty roast dinner swallowed down by a few beers.

He was still walking but very slowly and constantly lost his balance.

Chapter Sixteen – Tom's nutty days

As a child Tom was always up to mischief. He would never do anything nasty, to purposefully hurt anyone, but he was a clown. He had the ability to make people laugh by doing daft things.

One day I couldn't find him in the garden and called for him everywhere. The garden was enclosed with a gate and I had seen him go out the back, so I knew he had to be there somewhere.

I called Jeff and told him Tom was missing. Jeff immediately went into the back garden and shouted for him. Robyn was also in the back garden and I saw her look up at a massive tree we had at the bottom of the garden. OMG! No way.

I shouted again and this time, about thirty feet up, I saw Tom's head poke out at the top of the tree! He waved at me.

Jeff went scooting up but couldn't get very far so ended up coaxing Tom down.

He never did climb that tree again, but one day he chose to climb the large front tree. My father had been taken ill in Cyprus and Jeff had to drive me to the airport at Exeter. Jeff would be gone two hours. We left the kids, now fourteen and eleven, and went off. I called a friend on the way and asked him to go over to watch the kids until Jeff got back.

In the thirty minutes it took him to arrive, Tom had climbed up the front tree and Robyn had followed. Tom lost his footing and fell but landed on something soft, so he was fine.

Unfortunately, the something soft was Robyn, and she was knocked out of the tree and knocked out on a brick wall.

Neighbours rallied around and when Robyn wouldn't regain consciousness an ambulance was called.

By the time Jeff arrived home the ambulance was leaving. Luckily Robyn wasn't in it and they had deemed her fine to rest and recover at home.

Tom blamed Robyn and Robyn blamed Tom.

Tom was so accident prone as a child. He broke his ankle on a neighbour's trampoline, and then broke a toe when he hit it with his crutch after trying to go too fast.

He broke his ankle again after falling over a wall running for a bus. He dislocated a shoulder after going down a slide with his nephew Oliver.

He broke his hand when he hit someone or something.

When Ashley Tossell, his favourite PE teacher, died suddenly, the whole town went into mourning. With the help of two local footballers we decided to hold a football tournament in his honour and raise some money for the charity of his family's choice.

I split everyone into teams including girls and boys so it was mixed. It was played at the all-weather pitch at Tavistock College and they generously let us have it for nothing. Toilet facilities were also donated and a burger van arrived. It was all looking good. Referees volunteered their services

It started well and Ashley's son played in the tournament with old and current pupils. There was only one calamity of the day. Yep! Tom.

I saw someone go down on the far pitch and then I heard Robyn say, "Mum, it's Tom!"

Thinking he had a seizure I went rushing over, but when I saw him smiling I knew it wasn't a seizure. "Mum, I'm fine," he said. "But I think my arm is broken."

And after an X-ray it showed that it was.

When he was able to go back to work he sliced himself with a screwdriver and severed a tendon, got an infection and ended up in hospital again!

Tom loved the moors and loved taking Josh up there and show him the beautiful scenery of Dartmoor.

He loved scrambling up Tors and climbing, and one day he decided to show Josh how to get across a small river using a long branch on a tree. As he was doing his possum act the branch broke and he fell straight into the river. Luckily Jess was filming it and now it is just one of his funny memories.

Chapter Seventeen –
One's burden

My burden is stress. When I am stressed, I drink. When I am happy, I drink. Now I am not happy. I am very sad and cannot contemplate ever being happy again. Yet still I drink.

I realise drink dependency is an illness. Sometimes I think if I had a terminal illness how would I react?

Would I be grateful that soon my misery and loss would be over? Probably not.

Would I be as brave as Jeff and Tom and come to some sort of acceptance that it was going to happen and it is what it is? Probably not.

Would I feel sorry for myself and be kicking and screaming about the unfairness of it all? Probably.

Therefore, why am I taking myself to an early grave? I'm intelligent enough to know that drinking two bottles of prosecco a night is not doing my health any good. The weight is piling on with all those extra calories and every morning I hate myself. I feel guilty, I feel fat and bloated, and I have an upset stomach.

I make a vow to myself. Right, today I am not going to have a drink. But late afternoon something happens and I drink. Is it the evenings I can't get through? I go to bed at 9pm so it's not late. So what is it?

Yes, drink makes me feel relaxed but can also make me very agitated. I can't go out of an evening due to drink, so I just shut myself away with my two dogs.

I prefer to drink alone.

I don't get falling down drunk but I know the amount I drink would poleaxe most people. I don't say that proudly.

My mind is full of images during the day and full of vivid dreams during the night. Sometimes, they are so vivid I don't want to go back to sleep.

There is not an hour that goes by I don't think about Tom or Jeff, or both, and my father. Three dead relatives within ten months. There we are, an excuse to drink!

I manage two and a half days work a week as a housing officer. God knows how! But as my job share colleague Julie would say, it's a distraction.

Yes, it is, but I also must deal with tenants who complain about the tiniest thing, like a small crack in a wall or they think a boundary is two inches into their property. I also deal with people Tom's age who have never worked, take drugs and expect a roof over their head but live in a pigsty.

It's not easy to deal with and I can only thank my partner Julie for her support as I would never be able to cope.

There is always an excuse to drink. I've had a stressful day. I've had a good day. I'm feeling sad today. I'm feeling happy today. Family are coming for drinks and food. Family aren't coming.

The sun is out so it must be prosecco time. It's raining so let's have a glass of red wine.

Physical issues don't help. My back hurts and my right ankle is as bad as the left one when I had an operation.

What I should be thinking is I've had a stressful day, let's have a nice walk with the dogs, and a hot bath.

I've had a good day today, let's have a nice walk with the dogs and put a film on.

I'm feeling sad today, let's have a cup of herbal tea and if I need to cry just cry.

I'm feeling happy today, let's have a cup of herbal tea and find something funny to laugh at.

Family are coming, let's all go for a drive onto the moors and have a family walk while a roast is cooking.

The family aren't coming. Get off your lazy ass and do some outstanding jobs.

The sun is out, let's get off your lazy ass and do some much needed gardening.

It's raining, lets make a start on all those inside jobs.

Yeah, right! In a perfect world.

I have put on nearly four stone since the first death and it's mainly down to drinking alcohol and then eating junk food.

Would losing that four stone make me feel happier about myself? Yes, it would, and maybe my back wouldn't hurt so much and I could get some weight off my poor ankle.

I wouldn't feel so bloated or tired. I would have more energy. I would feel better about myself. I would have more confidence. I wouldn't have upset stomachs all the time. I would feel better.

So, why am I making myself miserable? I wish I knew the answer.

Chapter Eighteen –
St Luke's again and lockdown

Tom started his chemotherapy, which we all knew was going to be a strong one and make him feel very poorly. As if he couldn't feel any more poorly.

Jess took him into Derriford and stayed with him. He fell asleep during the process, but after it was finished they couldn't wake him up.

They moved him to a ward and Jess was told he would need more tests.

Tom's health continued to deteriorate and he didn't fully understand where he was and why he couldn't go home. It was heart breaking to see my son so distressed.

After a few days on a ward we were told he was going to be moved to St Luke's Hospice again.

I think I knew deep down that this was the last move he was going to have, and he wouldn't be coming home this time.

We all tried to explain to Josh how poorly his dad was, but because he had come home last time I don't think he believed us.

Then lockdown arrived. It took us all by surprise and nobody could comprehend how this was going to affect us.

My darling son was in a hospice receiving end of life care. We would obviously be exempt.

In "we" I meant all his family. His mum, his sister, his wife and his two children. I did appreciate why his friends couldn't visit.

Then one day Poppy's nursery called Jess to say Poppy had a high temperature and could she pick her up from nursery. Unfortunately, Jess was at Derriford speaking with a St Luke's nurse who picked up on the conversation.

That was it! Jess and Poppy could no longer visit Tom. Jess began to feel unwell too but was adamant it was just a cold.

We tried the doctor's surgery and literally begged to have them both tested, but we were refused. The surgery did everything possible but government guidelines had to be adhered to. No testing.

I remember that Jess and Robyn were with me when we got the call to say Jess and Poppy couldn't visit anymore. I'd had a few proseccos but I went ballistic with the poor doctor. I was crying and I remember someone screaming, then realised it was me.

Jess calmly took the phone off me and said she understood and thanked the doctor for trying to help.

I was in pieces. My son was dying and they wouldn't let him see his wife or daughter. It was disgraceful.

Tom wouldn't understand why. He didn't understand about Covid. He would think they didn't care anymore. It broke my heart.

The following day I went in to see Tom with Robyn. We had to wash our hands but didn't have to wear face masks.

Tom was in a ward but the only one in it. It looked huge and poor Tom looked lost and lonely in it.

We tried to explain why Jess and Poppy couldn't visit now because of Covid but he seemed confused.

A doctor arrived and said he needed to speak to Tom frankly. I braced myself but I didn't expect it to be quite so brutal.

He told Tom that there was no more treatment possible. He told him it was only a matter of time. He told him he could have as much pain relief as he wanted and when he wanted it. There was no limit.

61

Tom asked about the special really strong chemo that he was due to have as he was forever hopeful, but the doctor told him he'd had one dose and this was why he was back in St Luke's.

The doctor then asked him if he understood what he was saying. By this time Robyn and I had tears running down our faces.

The doctor pressed on and asked Tom if he understood there was no more treatment on offer.

I could barely see Tom through my tears, but I saw him nod.

I dropped Robyn home and drove home in a blur. I don't even remember the journey back.

Robyn had kept repeating, that was brutal. And she was right. Maybe necessary but brutal.

I drunk myself into a stupor that night and was so confused the next day I wasn't even sure if I had dreamt it.

Chapter Nineteen – The strength of a wife

We fully updated Jess but she wasn't about to give up and not see Tom again, or not let Tom see his beloved daughter.

Jess decided to contact St Luke's and ask if Tom could be put in a wheelchair and taken to the front room where they could see him through a window.

I will never forget the photo Jess took that evening. Little Poppy looking up at her dad holding her hand out and Tom smiling down at her and holding his hand out, but a massive piece of glass blocking them from touching.

I had to do something. This just wasn't right.

Trouble was, with Covid lockdown rules there was nothing I could do. I felt so helpless.

So maybe just have some more to drink and dull the pain. I wish I didn't detest drugs so much as I would have probably been on them as well!

The schools had shut down so Josh was free most days. I picked him up one day and we travelled to St Luke's. I didn't know that this was the last time before they shut St Luke's down for visitors as well.

Josh and I had to wear a mask and gloves and go through questions and a hand wash.

We found Tom all by himself in a ward. He looked so lonely and lost. We tried to explain that Jess and Poppy couldn't visit but I don't think he really understood.

By this time he was not mobile at all and the whole of his left side, including his handsome face, wasn't working.

He smiled his lop-sided smile at Josh and Josh chatted away telling him all the stuff he had got up to. It wasn't long though when Tom started to drift off and I could see he was fighting sleep.

We kissed him goodbye and told him we would come back again tomorrow.

This wasn't to be. St Luke's closed for visitors.

Tom couldn't see any text messages as his eyesight had become so poor. He couldn't answer his mobile as he couldn't see what button to press. He was now totally isolated and he didn't know why. It was killing me.

I decided I would write him a letter and arranged with St Luke's that when the letter arrived someone would read it out to him. I wanted him to know what a happy childhood he had. I wanted him to know about all our wonderful holidays. I wanted him to know that he had two very special children who would do him proud. I wanted to tell him that although his life had been cut short, he had achieved so much and enjoyed every second of it. Most of all, I wanted to tell him how much his dad and I had loved him.

It was such a difficult letter to write and it took ages as my eyes kept filling with tears.

I rang St Luke's a couple of days later and they confirmed they had read the letter to Tom.

I don't know what the reason was, it may have been Jess's evening visits to a window outside St Luke's. It may have been conversations with doctors. I don't know.

Tom was coming home again.

An orthopaedic bed was set up in the front room and a stairlift was put in along with other stuff. Plus, a wheelchair as Tom could no longer walk.

All his medication came with him and nurses popped in daily.

Jess was amazing! She had made every decision and she had got it spot on. Everything she did she did with Tom's best intentions.

She not only had Poppy to care for but also Tom. She took him to the toilet, fed and watered him and kept him company.

I looked at her one day through an open window (due to Covid restrictions) and thought you are the most amazing person I have ever met.

Tom didn't understand Covid restrictions and why he could not give me a hug or see his friends.

In the end Covid went out the window.

I needed to give my boy a hug. I needed to speak with him.

Chapter Twenty – Poppy's second birthday and the end

On Sunday 19th April 2020 Poppy turned two. She was incredibly resilient and had sleepovers with people she didn't really know. Poppy loved everyone! She was beautiful. Everyone loved Poppy.

Jess threw a little party outside and friends came and went but didn't stay long.

Tom managed a rum and Coke and then got hungry, so Jess made him some food and he went back to bed. He was so tired all the time.

Josh came and played with Poppy in a little paddling pool and all in all it was a good day.

Little did we know a week later was going to be the worst day of my life.

By this time I had gone sick from work so I could spend as much time with Tom as I could. Having said that it wasn't easy seeing your son so poorly with no quality of life whatsoever.

Jess held up better than me and Robyn was there for extra support, especially with Poppy.

However, friends were queuing up to look after Poppy because everyone loved her.

So, a week later on Sunday 26th April 2020 I rode my scooter down to visit. After a big hug from Poppy I saw that Kay, Jess's mum, was down, and she explained that she was going to stay with Tom and Jess.

I was so pleased her mum was staying. She had been an absolute rock the first time Tom had been taken into hospital.

Tom was asleep but didn't seem comfortable. He kept rolling around on the bed and it was obvious he was in pain.

Jess rang the nurse and it wasn't long before she came. Her name was Jane and I knew her. I knew that she had lost a son. I knew that she had a daughter who struggled looking after her children and she would have them a lot when she wasn't working. I had met her before when I was manager of a small homeless hostel and her daughter had been a nightmare. She was eventually evicted.

I thought things might be tense but they weren't. She was a true professional. She explained that Tom was dying and his body was shutting down. It was difficult to hear, even when we knew it was happening. Tom was going to leave us today and I would never be able to speak to him again. I was never going to see his lovely smile again. I was losing my son, and there was nothing I could do about it.

I don't know who opened the first bottle of prosecco, probably me. After that people came and went. Friends travelling down from Newcastle, London and Bristol. All to say their goodbyes to their mate who they loved.

The whole day was a blur of people coming and going. Jess had rung Josh's mum and he was adamant he wanted to come and see his dad. He was only nine and so brave.

As he came in I could see he had been crying and when he held his daddy's hand he couldn't stop sobbing. I thought my heart was going to break.

Luckily there were friends there who talked to Josh, and it wasn't long before he was playing with Poppy and chatting to everyone.

I took him for a little walk up the road and we passed the police station, the fire station and the ambulance station. We had a chat about all his fond memories and all the fun stuff he had done with his daddy.

By now people had gone down to the local shop and bought more prosecco and some crisps for us to nibble on.

The day wore on and soon it was late afternoon. My brother had arrived and I could see he was shocked with everything that was happening. Tom now had a driver into his arm, which was an immediate and constant pain relief and he looked peaceful and didn't look like he was in pain. His breathing was ragged and I could see it was an effort to breathe.

Jess and I had discussed about donating organs, and it would have been wonderful for someone to have Tom's heart, lungs, kidneys and liver. It would be some comfort to know that he had saved other people's lives and some of his body would live on.

However, that wasn't an option as Tom had had too much chemo and his vital organs would have been damaged.

Everyone took it in turns to hold his hand and speak to him.

It was a glorious sunny day and people sat outside talking quietly together and drinking and some smoking.

A lot of friends had said their goodbyes and left, so early evening there was just me, Robyn and James, my brother Hugh, Jamie and Ashley and Kay.

Jessie had taken a very tearful Josh home and Jess's best friend Taz had taken Poppy for the evening.

It was my turn to sit with Tom and hold his hand and I told him how much I loved him and how proud I was of him and how I would always look after Jess and his children.

I could hardly see anything as my eyes were so full of tears.

James was sat on the sofa next to me and suddenly Tom gripped my hand, opened his eyes and said, "Dad."

That was it! One word. Dad. I looked at James and asked him if he had heard that and he said he had.

I didn't know what to think. I wasn't religious. I didn't believe in life after death. But I heard it.

The day went on and turned into evening and Tom was still hanging in there. The nurse, Jane, had hardly left our sides. She was due to finish soon but said she would stay. She kept checking Tom's pain relief and was topping it up with injections.

I don't know what she thought of us as we had all continued drinking throughout the afternoon.

I had probably drunk the most. The whole scene of looking at Tom dying in an orthopaedic bed was turning into a dreamlike state, and part of me thought that what was I was witnessing wasn't really happening.

If I don't say goodbye to him he won't go.

But he did. Jess called out and we all went in. I can't even remember who else was with Jess when Tom stopped breathing, but we were all by his bed within seconds.

The first thing that dawned on me was Tom's chest wasn't moving. I don't know why I had to do it but I felt for his pulse and Ashley felt for his neck pulse.

Bloody stupid! It was obvious that my beautiful, caring, wonderful son, husband and daddy had gone. He had left us.

The rest was a blur of my brother trying to get me home and saying something about eating. I didn't want to eat! I wanted to drink myself into oblivion.

I didn't wait for the undertakers. Jess chose the same ones that had collected Jeff.

My beautiful brave daughter helped Jane clean and wash Tom and redress him. To this day I don't know how she had the strength to do that.

I was finished. I don't even remember the rest of the evening. I was just grateful that Kay was going to stay with Jess, and I had my brother.

Chapter Twenty-one –
The bond of father and son

I remember hearing once that anyone with a bit of sperm can be a father, but being a dad takes love and hard work.

When Jeff became a dad he cried. He changed nappies, he got up in the night to feed him. He cuddled him after a fall and read him stories.

If we went to a pub for a meal, Tom came with us in his carrycot. He came with us on every holiday. He was part of the family and family went everywhere together.

Jeff's job was stressful and with long unsociable hours it was difficult to always be around at bedtimes.

However, on a day off he would spend all his time with Tom and they adored each other.

When Robyn came along three years later Jeff cried again. He looked at her beautiful face and her mass of dark curly hair, and I could see this one was going to have Daddy around her little finger.

Jeff was lucky with the police force and when his service was completed he retired. He had a good pension and he never did a paid job again. The kids were six and nine. That was when we travelled around Canada for a month.

Jeff would take the kids to school and pick them up again. He played with them constantly. He was desperate to get Tom into rowing but he wasn't interested. It was football, football, football! Much to my delight.

Jeff was there when Tom got drunk at the age of sixteen and threw up everywhere.

Jeff taught Tom to drive. He bought him his first little car. Jeff sorted the car out when Tom wrote it off! Jeff sorted everything out when Tom crashed the courtesy car.

Jeff loaned him the money to buy a new car.

Jeff cried first when Tom said he was going to be a father.

We both cried when we saw our little grandson, Josh, for the first time.

Jeff was with him when the surgeon told him he had a brain tumour. He was with him during his epilepsy appointments. He was with him in London when he had an operation to remove eighty per cent of the tumour.

He was also with him when he had a course of radiotherapy and then chemotherapy.

He went to London every few months with Tom for his scans and consultant appointments.

He rang me straightaway to say the tumour hadn't grown or changed. I could carry on as normal then, until the next scan, when the worry and stress started all over again.

Jeff was so happy when he met and married Jess, and then the birth of little Poppy a few months later saw a very happy contended dad and grandad.

Jeff wasn't there the night Tom died. He had died nine months before his son.

For that I am grateful.

Chapter Twenty-two –
Stress is definitely a killer

The bond of father and daughter used to be strong, but when my father arrived back into the UK from Cyprus the nightmare began.

He had fallen out with the next door neighbours who virtually did everything for him.

He had moved out to Cyprus with my mum fifteen years ago and had been happy there. Their social life had been amazing. They had four close English neighbours and there was always something going on.

They would be entertained or entertaining virtually every night.

We would visit every year and the kids loved it there. They would virtually live in the neighbours' pool or we would take them to the beach and various historic sites.

Paphos was a beautiful place and they both seemed very happy there.

Then my mum died. My brother and I went out and brought them both home. My mum was buried in Mawnan Smith old church overlooking the sea. It was the church where Jeff and I had been married and both children had been christened.

Father did return to Cyprus but he came back often and we went out often.

Father had always been a heavy drinker, and now Mum was gone it got worse.

Funny how that passed down to me when I lost my husband.

My drinking progressively got worse. Jeff would nag me if I drank a whole bottle of wine during an evening, now I was on two!

I wouldn't normally drink on a work day, but now my work days were only two and a half a week it gave me more drinking nights.

Also, Sundays seem to have become family lunch days. So, I could hardly do lunch for everyone without some alcohol.

Then when I managed to work on a Monday I thought I might as well have a drink Monday night as I only had to work Tuesday morning. So, the only night I wasn't drinking was Tuesday. I had Josh for tea every other Tuesday and had to drop him home after, so that became the one night I didn't drink.

I knew it should be the other way around and just have one drinking night.

There was always an excuse though. What a lovely, happy family day – lets drink.

No one is coming this weekend – let's drink.

I am in a reasonably good mood, so I'll have a drink.

I'm in a terrible mood, so I'll have a drink.

When father arrived we set him up in a two-bed apartment by the Tavy river. It was a lovely little place and close to the shops.

We unpacked all the boxes that had been shipped over from Cyprus and set him up with everything he would need.

It wasn't enough! My dear husband took him to every hospital visit, every GP visit and took him shopping and out to lunch.

Father became a burden on both of us and never seemed grateful for what we did.

In short, it wore Jeff down, but I didn't realise how much. I should have.

Jeff had also fallen out with one of his sisters (not Sara) and he was finding it hard dealing with her regarding his mother's will and property.

I am convinced to this day that stress was a major part in both the death of my husband and my son.

He was fit and healthy prior to this stress, and Tom also seemed well and was coping with his job and young family.

The stress of seeing his father dying in such horrid circumstances triggered something in the benign tumour, to change it to incurable brain cancer within weeks of his father's death.

It made me angry to think that it may have been caused by other people's thoughtless actions.

I did have it out with Father one day after a few nerve calming drinks.

To this day I don't think he thought that he had been the cause of all the stress. The arrogance of the man made me hate him.

He was my father; I didn't want to hate him. I wanted to love him and look after him.

Father passed away a week after Tom.

I went down to visit him late one afternoon, leaving my family playing in the garden with Josh and Poppy.

Hugh was up and he said he'd walk the dogs if I went down to check on Father.

Father was in his orthopaedic bed and in a sit up position.

He didn't look well and it was obvious he was in pain. I checked his morphine capsules and noticed that none had been given to him today. I took one out and asked him if he wanted one and he nodded. I gave it to him and then he said he was thirsty.

I gave him a sip of water and he was slightly sick. I went to get a cloth to clean him up, when a carer walked into the apartment.

She looked horrified to see me and said, "You have to go, he has Covid."

Time stood still for a minute as I just stared at her. I told her she was joking but she assured me he had been tested positive.

I washed my hands as best I could and explained to Father that I had to leave. He just looked at me.

When I got outside the apartment I rang Robyn and told her they would have to leave, go home and shower and wash all their clothes.

Hugh couldn't believe it. This was our worst fear. I was also angry that we hadn't been told. There was no way I would have gone down and put my family at risk had I known. It didn't make sense. Something didn't add up.

After a sleepless night I rang the GP at 9am. She checked the results and assured me my father did **not** have Covid. She was confused as to why the carer thought he had.

I immediately told Robyn and Jess and Josh's mum that it was fine and he didn't have Covid.

What a relief.

Five minutes later I had a call from a friend who lived in the same street to say there was an ambulance outside Father's apartment block. Now what?

Hugh was still in bed, so I drove down to the apartment to find an ambulance with two paramedics sat in it.

I went up to them and asked if they were here for David Clark. They confirmed they were but told me I couldn't go in as he had been tested positive for Covid.

I told them I had checked with the surgery and had been informed he had not been tested positive. One of the paramedics' phone rang and he answered it. It was the same GP that I had just spoken to, and I could tell by his demeanour that he was being told the correct position.

When he hung up he apologised and stated there had obviously been a mix up. He told me Doctor Robins was on her way down.

I asked him if I could go and see if my father was okay and if he needed anything and I will never forget his reply. "Oh sorry, he passed away during the night!"

So, my father was gone too. Alone, with no one holding his hand, because of that stupid carer.

Would I have stayed with him? If I knew he was dying that night of course I would! If not? Probably not.

I called Hugh and he came straight down, arriving at the same time as the doctor.

She knew of my losses and could hardly look at me. She just kept saying, "Sue, I'm so sorry."

She also said we didn't have to go in if we didn't want to, but we did. We needed to say goodbye.

He was still sat up in the same position as I had left him the night before. His complexion was ashen and grey. He looked awful! Not the vision I would have wanted as the last memory of my father.

Suddenly, I saw Jeff lying dead in his hospital bed on the busy ward. I saw Tom dead lying on his orthopaedic bed at home, and now my father and all their faces blurred into one.

I just started sobbing and had to sit down. I felt like I was going to die. I couldn't breathe so I got up again and went outside to breathe fresh air.

I stared down at the river running next to the apartment and tried to concentrate on the patterns and colours of the running water. I looked at some ducks and birds, but all I could see was faces.

Before I knew it the undertakers had arrived. The same ones for Jeff and Tom, and I could see the look of disbelief on their faces.

I didn't want sympathy. I didn't want a cuddle. I didn't want to talk. They were professional enough to just get on with their job.

Hugh and I left, agreeing to start cleaning the apartment out the next day.

I don't remember the rest of the day. It was a haze of drinking and nibbling at food. Also phoning family and friends.

I won't dwell on the cleaning and clearance of the place. It was a nightmare.

Luckily, Father had a few bottles of wine in the fridge which kept me going.

Robyn and James were a godsend and helped us clear everything out.

Chapter Twenty-three –
Tom's funeral

Friday 15th May 2020 was the day of my son's funeral. It should have been a massive affair but due to Covid rules only ten people could go to the crematorium at Bodmin.

Jess chose that crematorium because it was near Trevenna where they had got married, and she could look out at the same views.

The morning arrived and I went down to their house, located in a small close and very near the town.

Jess's mum was there plus a few close friends. When Josh arrived my heart broke for him.

I could see that he had been crying already, but he was so brave. There weren't many kids that age that could attend their dad's funeral. Especially so soon after his granddad's.

I held it together until the hearse arrived, a long black car that held my son's body. I just cried and cried and cried. No one could say anything that would make me feel better. I just wanted everyone to go away and leave me alone.

Then I looked out at the hearse parked up respectfully in the close, and I saw little Poppy staring into the hearse looking at the flowers on top of the coffin. She didn't understand her daddy was lying in the coffin. She was just fascinated with the beautiful flowers.

I knew then that I would get through this.

I knew that several people were going to line the road outside the house, but no one anticipated the huge number of people that wanted to say goodbye.

It started in the close and went all the way down the road and the road leading to the town. There must have been nearly three hundred people.

It was the most incredible thing I had ever witnessed. All these people, family and friends clapping for my boy. It was beautiful!

There were police standing outside the station, nurses standing outside the doctors' surgery and both sides of the road were full of clapping people. I looked at every one of them. I tried to smile but it was tough. As I'm writing this my eyes are full of tears, reliving that incredible moment.

James was driving my car with Jess in the front, and Robyn and I sat in the back. We followed the hearse that drove slowly and respectfully. Josh had gone on ahead with Jess's best friend Taz.

I wondered how Josh had reacted on seeing so many people. It would be an image he would have for the rest of his life.

The crematorium was about an hour away, and as we pulled up I could see why Jess had chosen this one. The setting was beautiful and peaceful.

The chosen ten people entered and I sat as close to Josh as I could. I looked at the coffin and pictured my son lying in it. It wasn't the best thing to do, and my eyes were so full of tears I couldn't see.

The vicar was the same one that Jeff had and he was lovely. He gave a lovely service and Jess managed her eulogy, showing everyone what an amazing brave person she is.

I managed to read a letter I had written to Tom when I had been unable to visit him at St Luke's due to Covid restrictions. It reminded him of all that he had done in his short life and the places he had visited. There were some funny anecdotes and people smiled.

The service wasn't long and we all had to leave without being able to touch the coffin to say our final goodbye.

Josh was in pieces and sobbing his heart out. His mum had come down to fetch him and he went running over to hug her. It was heart breaking.

Josh would come over to mine later as a few close friends and family were coming back for food and drink. We were all able to sit in the garden, but yes, Covid rules were broken. There was no way I wasn't going to give my son a send-off.

Sara and Mike had brought all the food down and had been preparing it all morning. It was a massive buffet and everyone soon tucked into the alcohol and food.

I sank two vodkas in about ten minutes.

Poor Jess was so tired she fell asleep for an hour on my sofa. We all left her alone and she felt better after her nap.

The evening soon came around and people started to leave apart from about five of Tom's friends who looked like they were going to stay all night.

I asked one friend if they could go soon as I was shattered. They respectfully left thanking me for allowing them to have a small get-together.

I fell into bed that night full of misery and alcohol.

Chapter Twenty-four –
Dates

My father's funeral five days later was a much smaller affair, with only one old friend turning up. A friend of Hugh's turned up and Hugh's three children and Robyn and me.

This was a burial at Mawnan Smith old church, near Falmouth which overlooked the Helford estuary.

The hearse arrived and once again I welled up. Too many funerals.

Again, we were not allowed to touch the hearse and father was wheeled down to the graveside by two undertakers.

The grave had already been dug up and my mother's headstone removed. I wondered briefly if she would be happy he was going in with her. He hadn't been the best of husbands and certainly not the best father.

I said a few words again and it was over. There was no wake and having said my goodbyes drove back to Tavistock.

The first date looming like a dark cloud of misery was 20th June, Jeff's birthday. It was a Saturday so Robyn, James, Jess and the grandchildren came around for lunch and to celebrate his birthday, and yes, there were a few drinks sunk that day.

On 2nd July was the first anniversary of my husband's death. Again, the family came to keep me company and again a few drinks were sunk.

On 10th August it was my sixty-first birthday, but it was a Monday so everyone came around on the Sunday. I remembered back to a year ago and the weekend at

Elfordleigh, Tom putting on his brave face making the day special despite knowing he was terminally ill.

It would have been our thirty-fifth wedding anniversary on 26th August. Poor Jeff. He never got any presents right. I know it used to stress him out. Birthdays were the hardest for him, but anniversaries weren't too bad. Flowers, champagne and a Chinese takeaway. It was a Wednesday so was pretty sure I'd spend it on my own, probably even working.

Tom and Jess's anniversary would have been 23rd September. He would have spoilt her rotten, as she deserved to be.

What did Jess do? She picked Josh up, bundled Poppy in her car and drove to Trevenna. She had packed a picnic and they ate it at the place the ceremony had taken place. I can't keep saying how amazing she is.

17th October would have been Tom's thirty-first birthday. It was a Saturday so once again the family came here for food and drink.

It was a very emotional day with laughter and tears. Tom would not want us to cry over him. He would want us to have a Morgan's for him and that's what we did. How could he drink that stuff? It was horrible!

On Friday 13th November Josh turned a big ten. Due to Covid he couldn't have a big party. I went over the top and bought him an electric mountain bike which he loved.

It was lovely seeing him ride it on the moors and smiling the whole time. I just loved seeing him happy. He had been through so much, losing two people he loved in such a short time.

Christmas rolled around and Robyn and James said they wanted to spend it with me. Jess and Poppy were going to a friend's house and would see me Boxing Day. Things didn't go quite as planned.

Jess's brother and family had visited just prior to Christmas and Grace, one of the daughters, had been poorly. When they returned home Grace was tested positive with Covid. So, poor Jess and Poppy had to self-isolate for two weeks and so did Josh as he had visited them. Christmas ruined.

Robyn, James and I had a good day playing silly games but they went home early evening. I watched some TV and went to bed. Another bad day over.

That's what days had become to me. Just get up, walk the dogs and get the day over so I could go back to bed.

If I didn't have the dogs, part of me thought I wouldn't bother getting out of bed. What was the point?

New Year's Eve arrived and because Hugh was staying for a few days decided to volunteer to have Josh and Poppy.

Luckily Robyn and James were in Tavistock that night so came up to help prior to bedtime.

Yes, I did have a few to drink but didn't overdo it because I had grandchildren.

At 3am my bedroom door swung open and through bleary eyes I saw Josh and Poppy standing there. Josh announced that Poppy had climbed into his bed and woken him up.

Okay, I thought. Climb in with me. I had Poppy next to me and then Josh beside her. Thank goodness I had a super king-size bed!

I listened to Poppy singing "Jingle bells" over and over and then suddenly all was quiet. Both had gone back to sleep. Unfortunately, I couldn't.

It didn't matter. I could not have been more content. I had my son's children all snuggled up next to me. I loved them so much. Josh was a mini Tom and Poppy a mini Jess. I felt peaceful in the knowledge that I would do my upmost to look after Tom's family. I had to stay healthy. I had to stop drinking!

There will always be dates in the calendar that are hard. There will always be times when grief will overwhelm you.

Friends who you think will stand by you don't. Some don't know what to say to you. Some will avoid you.

I get that. I am still working as a housing officer two and a half days a week. I don't want any further counselling. I don't need the friends who promised to stay in contact but haven't. I don't need to speak with someone daily. I am more than happy with my dogs.

What I do need are these people who have stayed in contact, not judged me, and accept me for being a recluse.

For accepting that yes, I do drink, but have also got it under control. I don't drink every day. I don't drink to excess. I don't want to die due to alcohol. One day I might give it up completely. One day I might buy a large camper van and just take off. Me and the dogs of course and on occasions Josh and Poppy.

I have plans now, which I didn't before. I want to live, which I didn't before. I have people who still need me and want me around.

The amount of grief I have been through must NOT define the person I am now. Wallowing in self-pity. Feelings of not existing. Feelings of battling through each day until it's over.

No more, Sue! Get your life together. You have people who love you. Some depend on you. Time to change forever! I know I am strong enough to do it. If I can survive this, I can survive anything.

People I want to thank:
Robyn Hammond
Jess Hammond
Josh Hammond
Poppy Hammond
Hugh Clark
James Burns
Sara Moss plus Harry and Jack
Mike Moss
Mandy Foster
Emma Perkins plus Billy and Ruby
Carl Austen
Sharon Tyler
Fran Grey
My neighbours
Cathy Veal
Mark Harris

Finally, my best mate Julie Harris. My job share partner and the one person who would never leave me on my own to become a recluse.

I know that I have the strength in me to do this. I know that total abstinence is not for me, but it's all about moderation and the belief that life is still worth living.

Having said that, I feel so much better, health wise without any alcohol. So maybe I won't ever drink again!

Not drinking has made me feel healthier, but it has also brought back the past and present. The last year has been such a blur, I feel I am now grieving all over again. Memories of their smiling faces are so vivid. The numbness has gone and now it's for real all over again. So, although I am crying a lot mourning my loss, I feel more positive.

Some people have an addictive gene, and I know I have it. At the moment, I can't stop cycling, working out and eating healthy. Even drinking Turmeric tea!

86

I also know that without the support of my family and close friends my addictive personality could go back to the alcohol.

I'm a nice person, but I'm not perfect!

Printed in Great Britain
by Amazon

67593689R00051